WHY DO DEAD FISH FLOAT?

learning about Matter with
THE GARBAGE GANG

by Thomas Kingsley Troupe

illustrated by Derek Toye

PICTURE WINDOW BOOKS
a capstone imprint

MEET THE GARBAGE GANG:

SAM HAMMWICH

Sam is a once-delicious sandwich that has a bit of lettuce and tomato. He is usually crabby and a bit of a loudmouth.

GORDY

Gordy is a small rhino who wears an eyepatch even though he doesn't need one. He lives in the city dump. His friends don't visit him in the smelly dump, so Gordy created his own friends—the Garbage Gang!

SOGGY

Soggy is a stuffed bear from a carnival game. She fell into a puddle of dumpster juice and has never been the same.

RICK

Rick is a brick. He is terrified of bugs, especially bees, which is odd . . . since he's a brick.

CANN-DEE

Cann-Dee is a robot made of aluminum cans. She can pull random facts out of thin air.

MR. FRIGID

Mr. Frigid is a huge refrigerator that sprouted arms and legs. He doesn't say much, but he's super strong.

3

Even I know that no one likes a dead fish sandwich.

Well, any fish sandwich is from a dead fish—just not rotten, stinky ones.

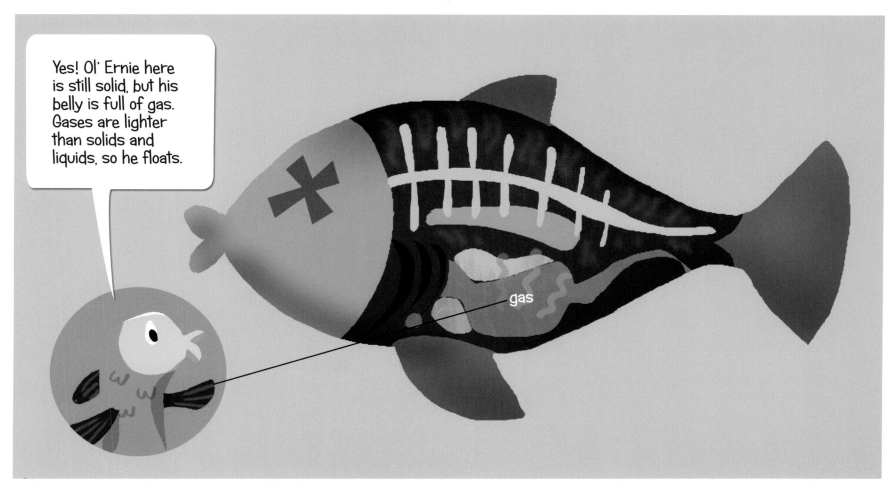

Glossary

You're looking up words? That's one smart move, kid!

atmosphere—the mixture of gases that surround Earth and some planets

carbon dioxide—a gas in the air that animals give off and plants use to make food

compress—to shrink

expand—to grow larger

lava—hot, liquid rock

matter—anything that has weight and takes up space: solids, liquids, and gases are the three kinds of matter

oxygen—a colorless gas that people breathe: humans and animals need oxygen to live

volume—the amount of space taken up by an object or substance

Read More

Braun, Eric. *Joe-Joe the Wizard Brews Up Solids, Liquids, and Gases.* In the Science Lab. Mankato, Minn.: Picture Window Books, 2012.

Monroe, Tilda. *What Do You Know About States of Matter?* 20 Questions. Physical Science. New York: PowerKids Press, 2011.

Walker, Sally M. *Investigating Matter.* How Does Energy Work? Minneapolis: Lerner Publications, 2012.

Incoming data suggests that books do not stink.

Critical Thinking Using the Common Core

1. There are three states of matter. Can you name examples of each state? How would each of your examples change into a different state? Use details to explain your answer. (Integration of Knowledge and Ideas)

2. Look at the diagram of Earth on page 17. How many states of matter do you see in the diagram? (Key Ideas and Details)

Index

Internet Sites

FactHound offers a safe, fun way to find Internet sites related to this book. All of the sites on FactHound have been researched by our staff.

Here's all you do:

Visit *www.facthound.com*

Type in this code: 9781479554799

Thanks to our advisers for their expertise, research, and advice:
Paul Ohmann, PhD, Associate Professor of Physics
University of St. Thomas

Terry Flaherty, PhD, Professor of English
Minnesota State University, Mankato

Editor: Shelly Lyons
Designer: Lori Bye
Art Director: Nathan Gassman
Production Specialist: Gene Bentdahl
The illustrations in this book were created digitally.
Picture Window Books are published by Capstone,
1710 Roe Crest Drive, North Mankato, Minnesota 56003
www.capstonepub.com

Library of Congress Cataloging-in-Publication Data
Cataloging-in-publication information is on file with the
Library of Congress
ISBN 978-1-4795-5479-9 (library binding)
ISBN 978-1-4795-5487-4 (eBook PDF)
Written by Thomas Kingsley Troupe
Illustrated by Derek Toye

Printed in the United States of America in North Mankato, Minnesota
032014   008087CGF14

Check out projects, games and lots more at
www.capstonekids.com
Super-cool stuff!

More books! Are you kidding me? This is the best news since sliced bread!

Seriously?

Look for all the books in the series:

DO ANTS GET LOST? Learning about Animal Communication with **THE GARBAGE GANG**

DO BEES POOP? Learning about Living and Nonliving Things with **THE GARBAGE GANG**

WHY DO DEAD FISH FLOAT? Learning about Matter with **THE GARBAGE GANG**

WHY DOES MY BODY MAKE BUBBLES? Learning about the Digestive System with **THE GARBAGE GANG**